TABLE OF CONTENTS

TABLE OF CONTENTS

#	SUBJECT	PAGE

TABLE OF CONTENTS

#	SUBJECT	PAGE

YEARLY CASH IN & CASH OUT SUMMARY

YEAR : ....

MONTH	CASH IN	CASH OUT	BALANCE	NOTES
TOTAL				

NOTES

YEARLY CASH IN & CASH OUT CHART

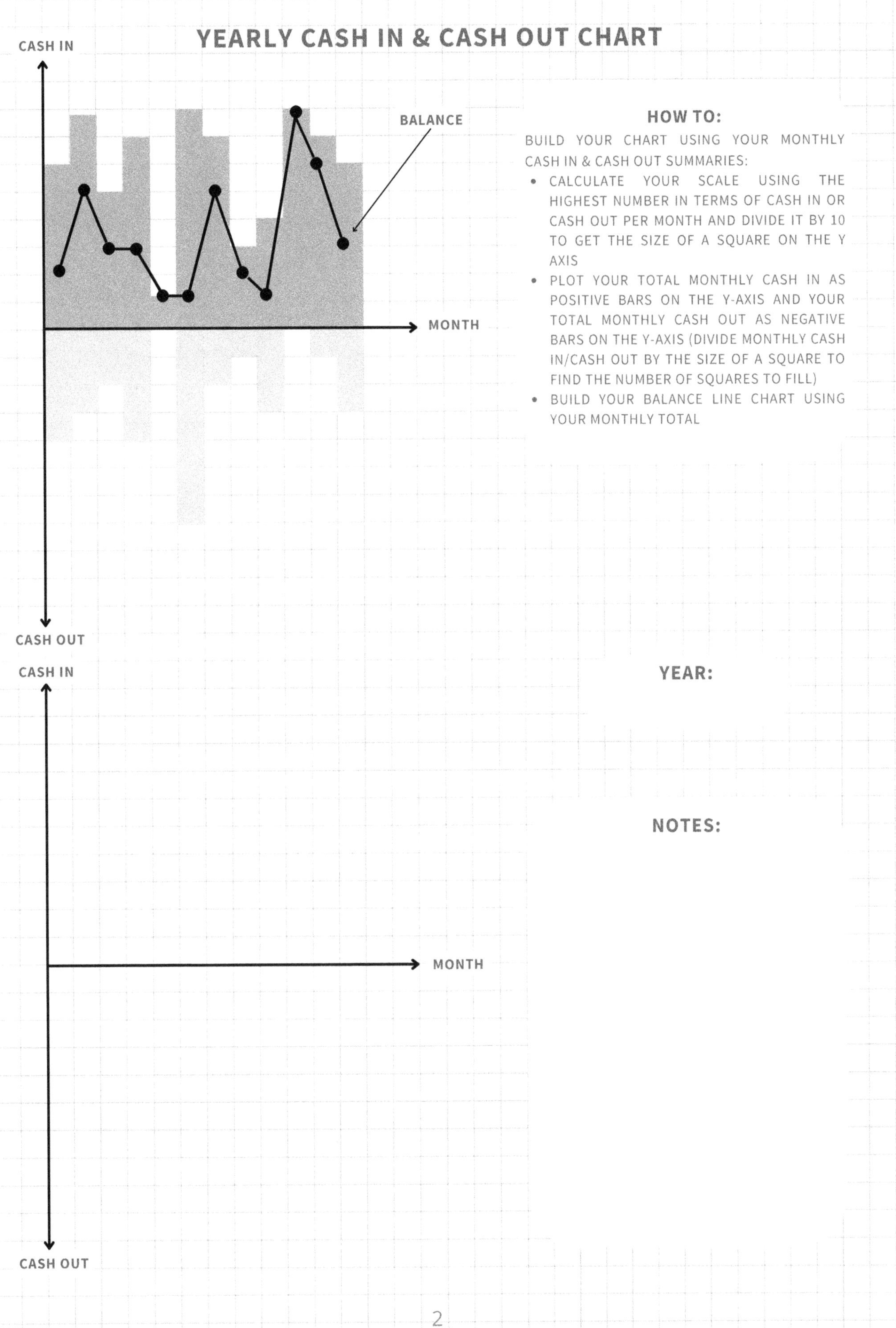

HOW TO:

BUILD YOUR CHART USING YOUR MONTHLY CASH IN & CASH OUT SUMMARIES:

- CALCULATE YOUR SCALE USING THE HIGHEST NUMBER IN TERMS OF CASH IN OR CASH OUT PER MONTH AND DIVIDE IT BY 10 TO GET THE SIZE OF A SQUARE ON THE Y AXIS
- PLOT YOUR TOTAL MONTHLY CASH IN AS POSITIVE BARS ON THE Y-AXIS AND YOUR TOTAL MONTHLY CASH OUT AS NEGATIVE BARS ON THE Y-AXIS (DIVIDE MONTHLY CASH IN/CASH OUT BY THE SIZE OF A SQUARE TO FIND THE NUMBER OF SQUARES TO FILL)
- BUILD YOUR BALANCE LINE CHART USING YOUR MONTHLY TOTAL

YEAR:

NOTES:

MONTHLY CASH IN & CASH OUT SUMMARY

MONTH : ....

DATE	DAY	CASH IN	CASH OUT	BALANCE	NOTES
1					
2					
3					
4					
5					
6					
7					
8					
9					
10					
11					
12					
13					
14					
15					
16					
17					
18					
19					
20					
21					
22					
23					
24					
25					
26					
27					
28					
29					
30					
31					
TOTAL					

MONTHLY CASH IN & CASH OUT CHART

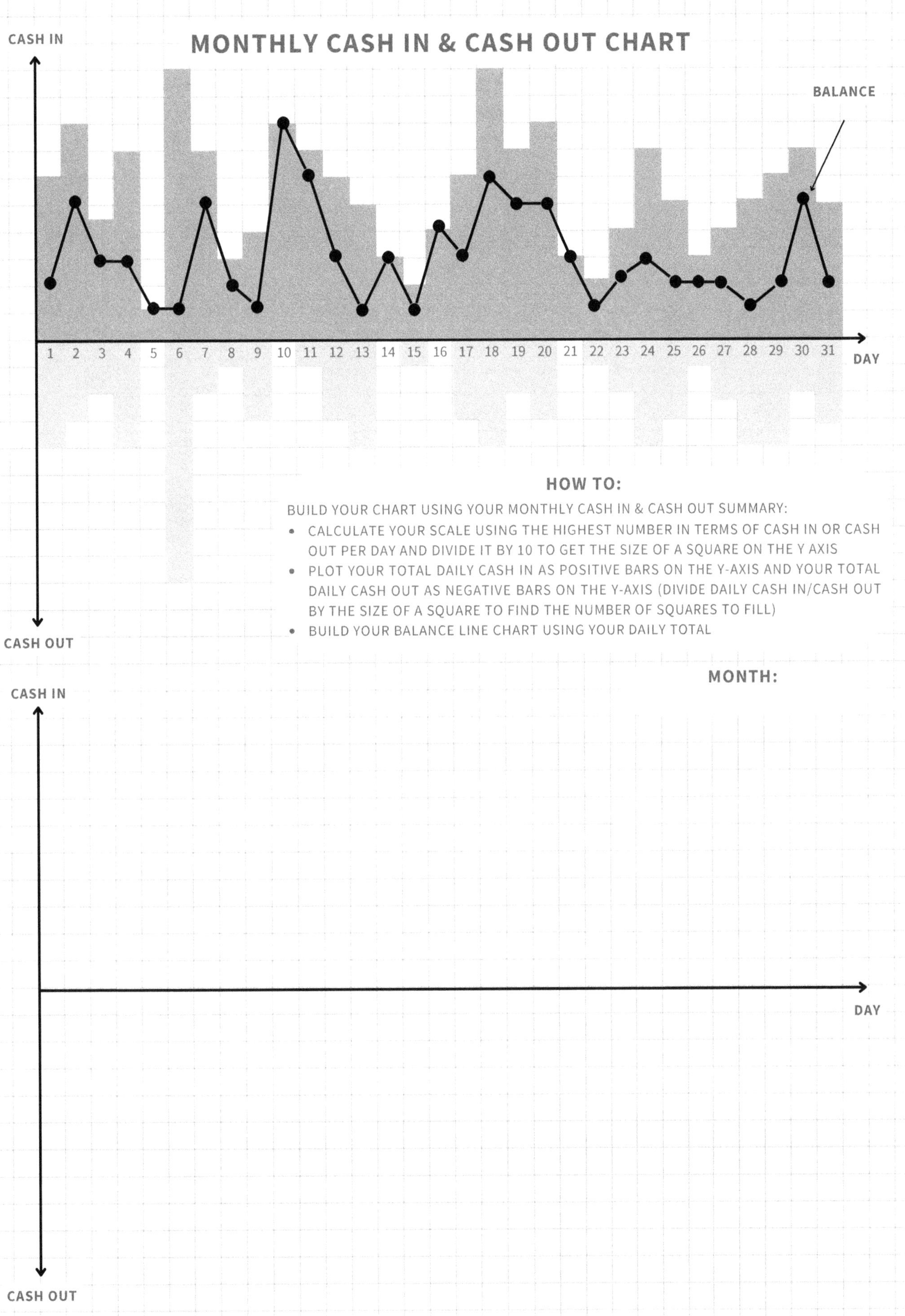

HOW TO:

BUILD YOUR CHART USING YOUR MONTHLY CASH IN & CASH OUT SUMMARY:

- CALCULATE YOUR SCALE USING THE HIGHEST NUMBER IN TERMS OF CASH IN OR CASH OUT PER DAY AND DIVIDE IT BY 10 TO GET THE SIZE OF A SQUARE ON THE Y AXIS
- PLOT YOUR TOTAL DAILY CASH IN AS POSITIVE BARS ON THE Y-AXIS AND YOUR TOTAL DAILY CASH OUT AS NEGATIVE BARS ON THE Y-AXIS (DIVIDE DAILY CASH IN/CASH OUT BY THE SIZE OF A SQUARE TO FIND THE NUMBER OF SQUARES TO FILL)
- BUILD YOUR BALANCE LINE CHART USING YOUR DAILY TOTAL

MONTH:

MONTHLY CASH IN & CASH OUT SUMMARY

MONTH : ....

DATE	DAY	CASH IN	CASH OUT	BALANCE	NOTES
1					
2					
3					
4					
5					
6					
7					
8					
9					
10					
11					
12					
13					
14					
15					
16					
17					
18					
19					
20					
21					
22					
23					
24					
25					
26					
27					
28					
29					
30					
31					
TOTAL					

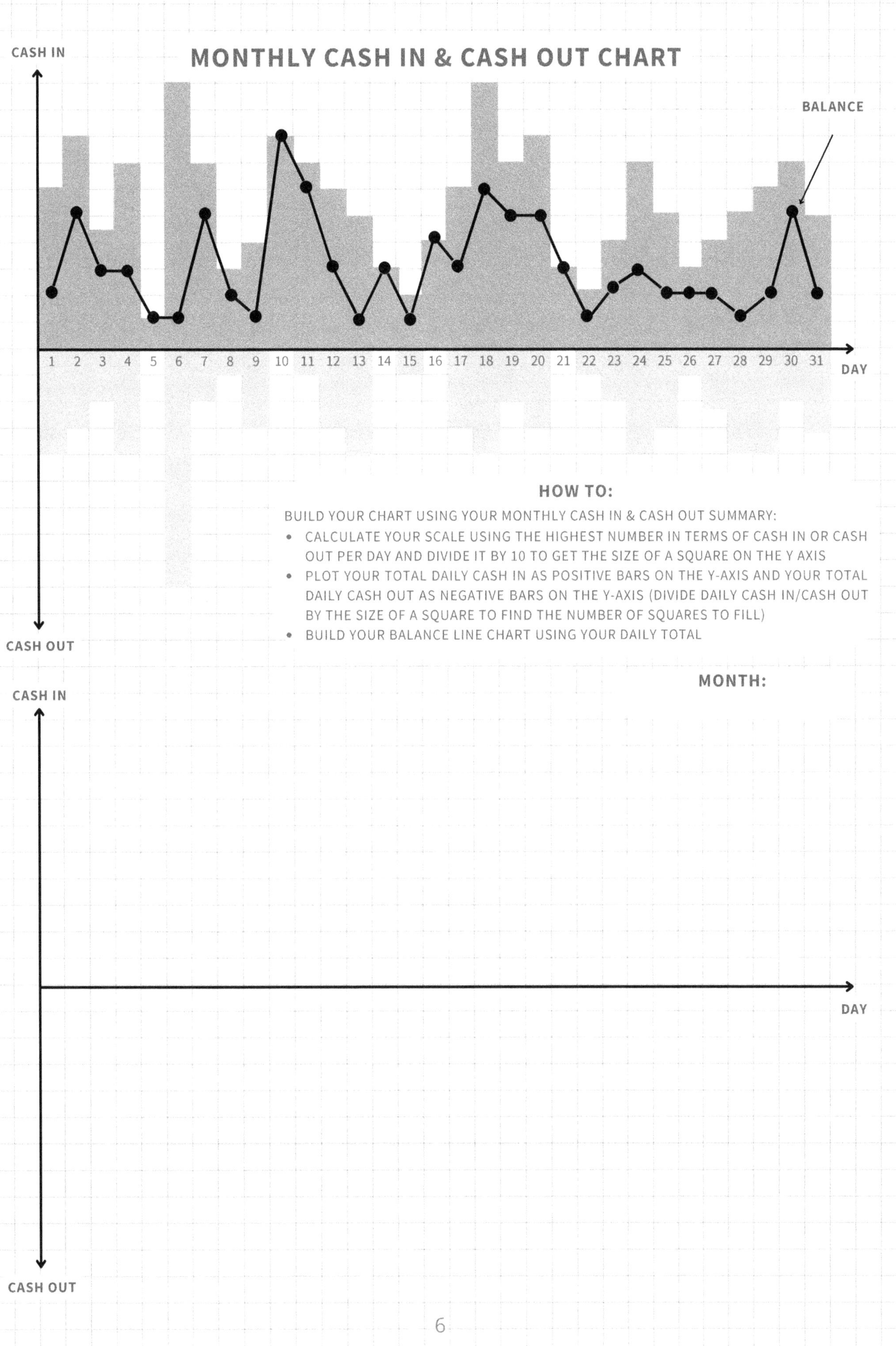
CASH IN
MONTHLY CASH IN & CASH OUT CHART
BALANCE
1 2 3 4 5 6 7 8 9 10 11 12 13 14 15 16 17 18 19 20 21 22 23 24 25 26 27 28 29 30 31
DAY
CASH OUT
HOW TO:
BUILD YOUR CHART USING YOUR MONTHLY CASH IN & CASH OUT SUMMARY:
• CALCULATE YOUR SCALE USING THE HIGHEST NUMBER IN TERMS OF CASH IN OR CASH OUT PER DAY AND DIVIDE IT BY 10 TO GET THE SIZE OF A SQUARE ON THE Y AXIS
• PLOT YOUR TOTAL DAILY CASH IN AS POSITIVE BARS ON THE Y-AXIS AND YOUR TOTAL DAILY CASH OUT AS NEGATIVE BARS ON THE Y-AXIS (DIVIDE DAILY CASH IN/CASH OUT BY THE SIZE OF A SQUARE TO FIND THE NUMBER OF SQUARES TO FILL)
• BUILD YOUR BALANCE LINE CHART USING YOUR DAILY TOTAL
MONTH:
CASH IN
DAY
CASH OUT

MONTHLY CASH IN & CASH OUT SUMMARY

MONTH : ....

DATE	DAY	CASH IN	CASH OUT	BALANCE	NOTES
1					
2					
3					
4					
5					
6					
7					
8					
9					
10					
11					
12					
13					
14					
15					
16					
17					
18					
19					
20					
21					
22					
23					
24					
25					
26					
27					
28					
29					
30					
31					
TOTAL					

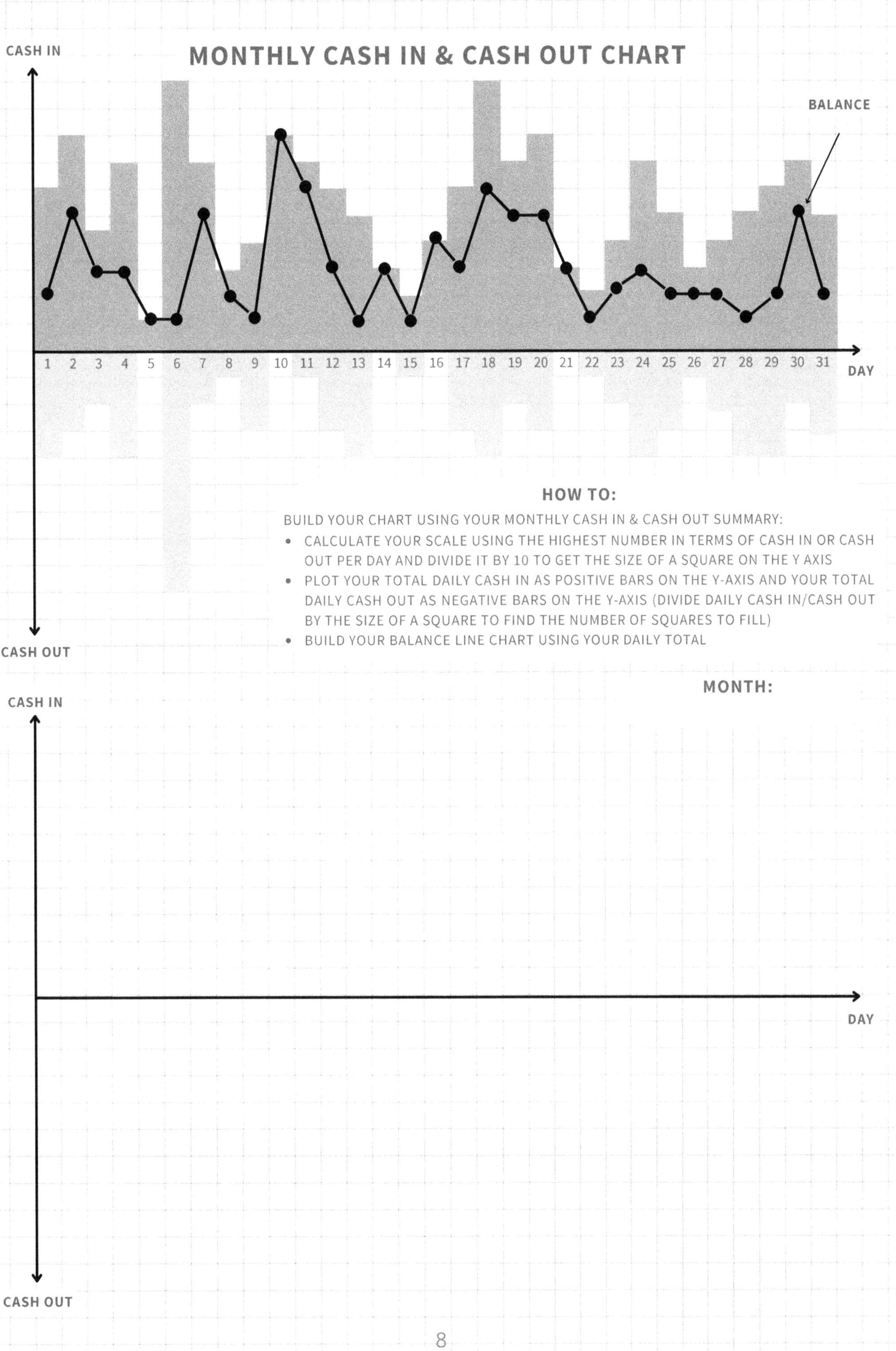
CASH IN
MONTHLY CASH IN & CASH OUT CHART
BALANCE
1 2 3 4 5 6 7 8 9 10 11 12 13 14 15 16 17 18 19 20 21 22 23 24 25 26 27 28 29 30 31
DAY
CASH OUT
HOW TO:
BUILD YOUR CHART USING YOUR MONTHLY CASH IN & CASH OUT SUMMARY:
• CALCULATE YOUR SCALE USING THE HIGHEST NUMBER IN TERMS OF CASH IN OR CASH OUT PER DAY AND DIVIDE IT BY 10 TO GET THE SIZE OF A SQUARE ON THE Y AXIS
• PLOT YOUR TOTAL DAILY CASH IN AS POSITIVE BARS ON THE Y-AXIS AND YOUR TOTAL DAILY CASH OUT AS NEGATIVE BARS ON THE Y-AXIS (DIVIDE DAILY CASH IN/CASH OUT BY THE SIZE OF A SQUARE TO FIND THE NUMBER OF SQUARES TO FILL)
• BUILD YOUR BALANCE LINE CHART USING YOUR DAILY TOTAL
MONTH:
CASH IN
DAY
CASH OUT

MONTHLY CASH IN & CASH OUT SUMMARY

MONTH : ....

DATE	DAY	CASH IN	CASH OUT	BALANCE	NOTES
1					
2					
3					
4					
5					
6					
7					
8					
9					
10					
11					
12					
13					
14					
15					
16					
17					
18					
19					
20					
21					
22					
23					
24					
25					
26					
27					
28					
29					
30					
31					
TOTAL					

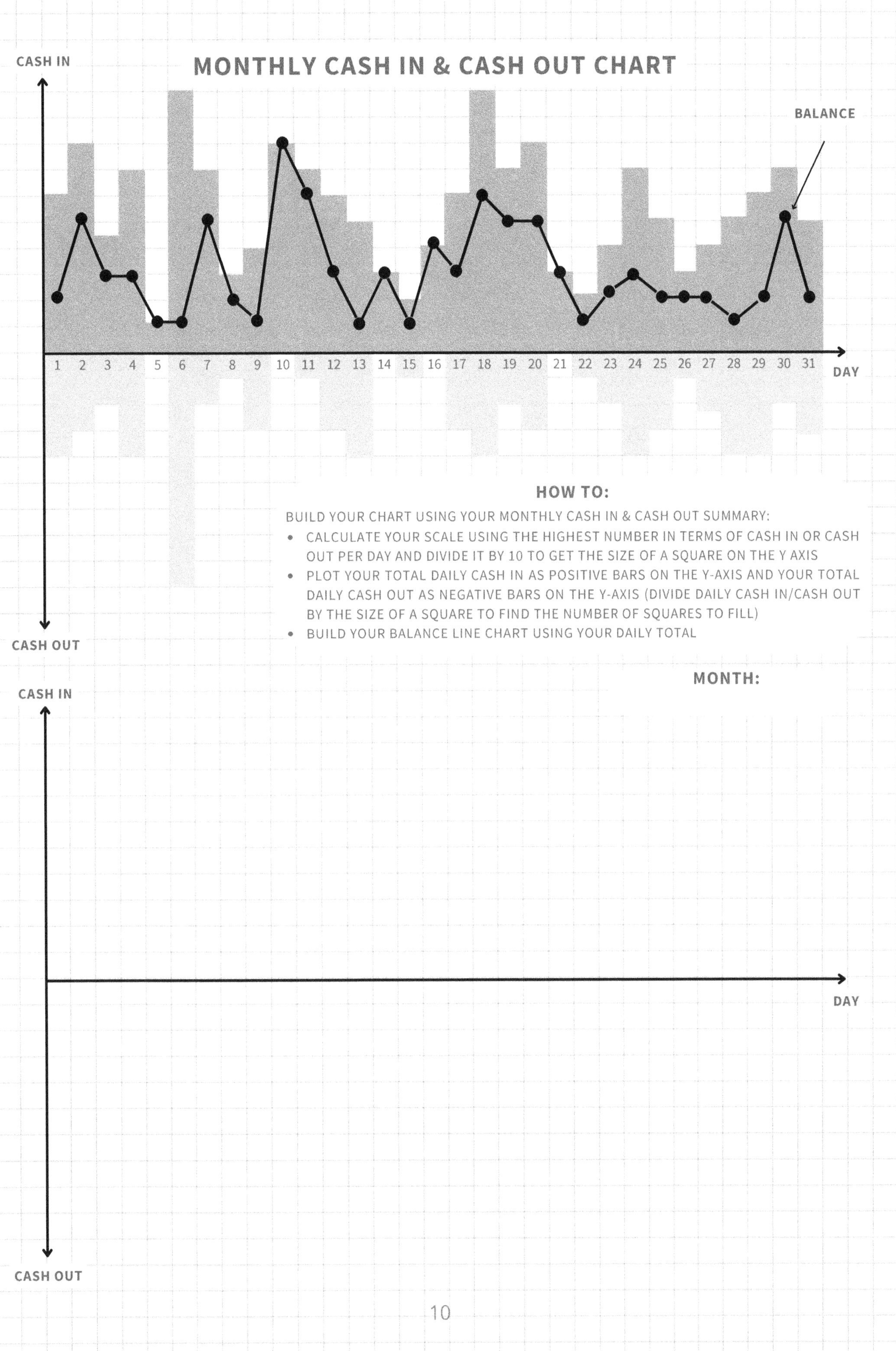

HOW TO:

BUILD YOUR CHART USING YOUR MONTHLY CASH IN & CASH OUT SUMMARY:

- CALCULATE YOUR SCALE USING THE HIGHEST NUMBER IN TERMS OF CASH IN OR CASH OUT PER DAY AND DIVIDE IT BY 10 TO GET THE SIZE OF A SQUARE ON THE Y AXIS
- PLOT YOUR TOTAL DAILY CASH IN AS POSITIVE BARS ON THE Y-AXIS AND YOUR TOTAL DAILY CASH OUT AS NEGATIVE BARS ON THE Y-AXIS (DIVIDE DAILY CASH IN/CASH OUT BY THE SIZE OF A SQUARE TO FIND THE NUMBER OF SQUARES TO FILL)
- BUILD YOUR BALANCE LINE CHART USING YOUR DAILY TOTAL

MONTH:

MONTHLY CASH IN & CASH OUT SUMMARY

MONTH : ....

DATE	DAY	CASH IN	CASH OUT	BALANCE	NOTES
1					
2					
3					
4					
5					
6					
7					
8					
9					
10					
11					
12					
13					
14					
15					
16					
17					
18					
19					
20					
21					
22					
23					
24					
25					
26					
27					
28					
29					
30					
31					
TOTAL					

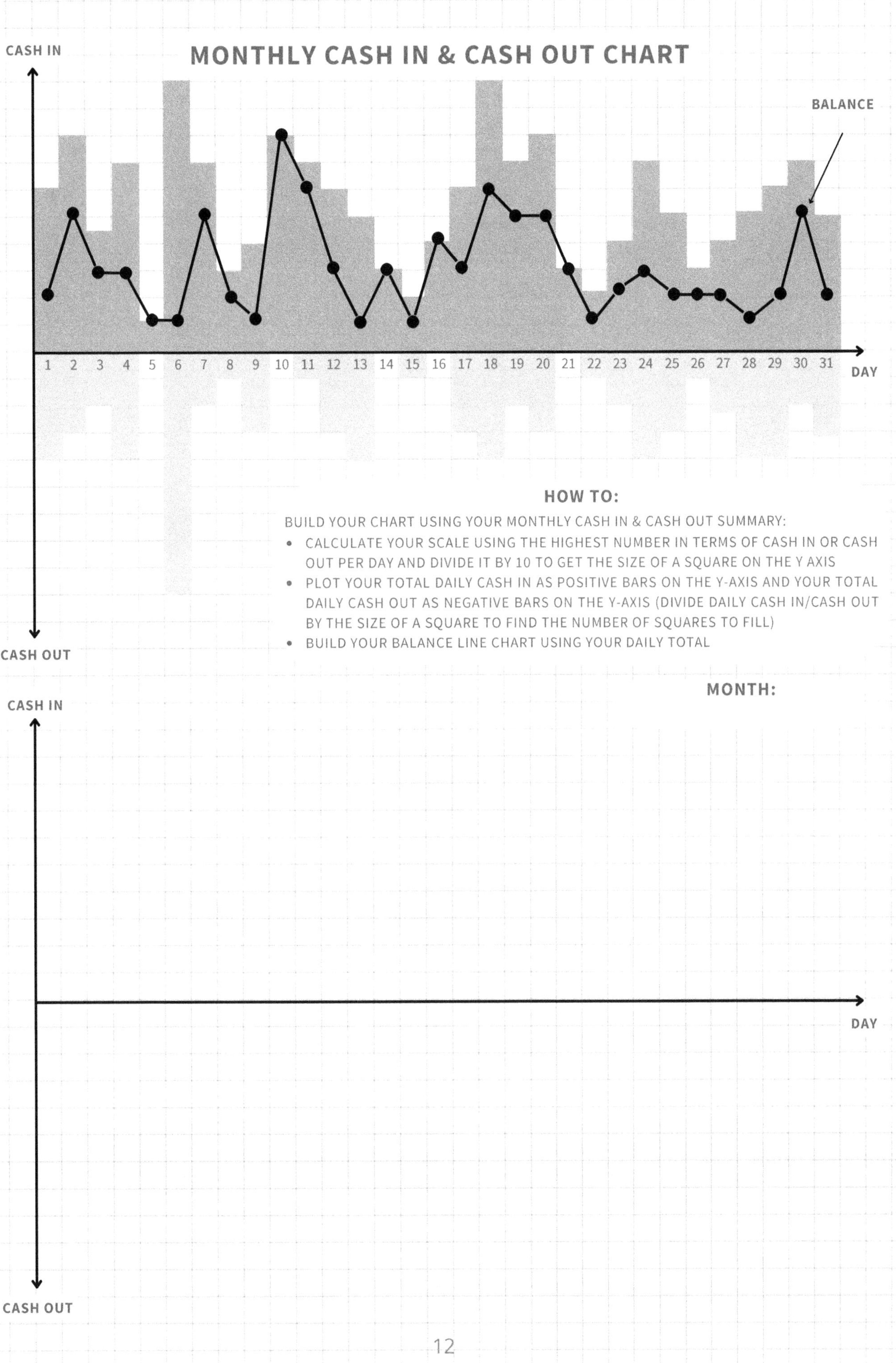

HOW TO:

BUILD YOUR CHART USING YOUR MONTHLY CASH IN & CASH OUT SUMMARY:

- CALCULATE YOUR SCALE USING THE HIGHEST NUMBER IN TERMS OF CASH IN OR CASH OUT PER DAY AND DIVIDE IT BY 10 TO GET THE SIZE OF A SQUARE ON THE Y AXIS
- PLOT YOUR TOTAL DAILY CASH IN AS POSITIVE BARS ON THE Y-AXIS AND YOUR TOTAL DAILY CASH OUT AS NEGATIVE BARS ON THE Y-AXIS (DIVIDE DAILY CASH IN/CASH OUT BY THE SIZE OF A SQUARE TO FIND THE NUMBER OF SQUARES TO FILL)
- BUILD YOUR BALANCE LINE CHART USING YOUR DAILY TOTAL

MONTH:

MONTHLY CASH IN & CASH OUT SUMMARY

MONTH : ....

DATE	DAY	CASH IN	CASH OUT	BALANCE	NOTES
1					
2					
3					
4					
5					
6					
7					
8					
9					
10					
11					
12					
13					
14					
15					
16					
17					
18					
19					
20					
21					
22					
23					
24					
25					
26					
27					
28					
29					
30					
31					
TOTAL					

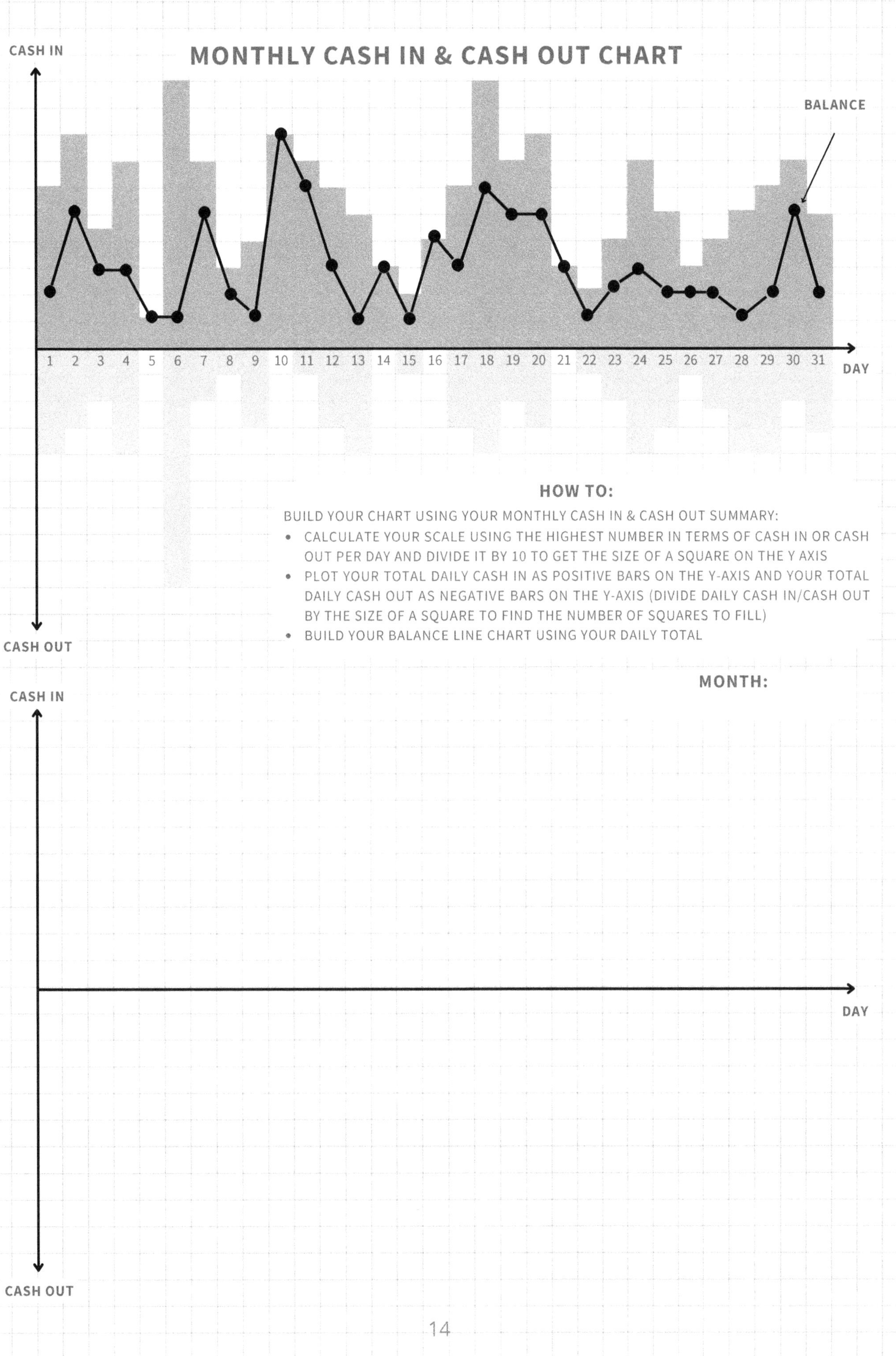
CASH IN
MONTHLY CASH IN & CASH OUT CHART
BALANCE
1 2 3 4 5 6 7 8 9 10 11 12 13 14 15 16 17 18 19 20 21 22 23 24 25 26 27 28 29 30 31
DAY
CASH OUT
HOW TO:
BUILD YOUR CHART USING YOUR MONTHLY CASH IN & CASH OUT SUMMARY:
• CALCULATE YOUR SCALE USING THE HIGHEST NUMBER IN TERMS OF CASH IN OR CASH OUT PER DAY AND DIVIDE IT BY 10 TO GET THE SIZE OF A SQUARE ON THE Y AXIS
• PLOT YOUR TOTAL DAILY CASH IN AS POSITIVE BARS ON THE Y-AXIS AND YOUR TOTAL DAILY CASH OUT AS NEGATIVE BARS ON THE Y-AXIS (DIVIDE DAILY CASH IN/CASH OUT BY THE SIZE OF A SQUARE TO FIND THE NUMBER OF SQUARES TO FILL)
• BUILD YOUR BALANCE LINE CHART USING YOUR DAILY TOTAL
MONTH:
CASH IN
DAY
CASH OUT

MONTHLY CASH IN & CASH OUT SUMMARY

MONTH : ....

DATE	DAY	CASH IN	CASH OUT	BALANCE	NOTES
1					
2					
3					
4					
5					
6					
7					
8					
9					
10					
11					
12					
13					
14					
15					
16					
17					
18					
19					
20					
21					
22					
23					
24					
25					
26					
27					
28					
29					
30					
31					
TOTAL					

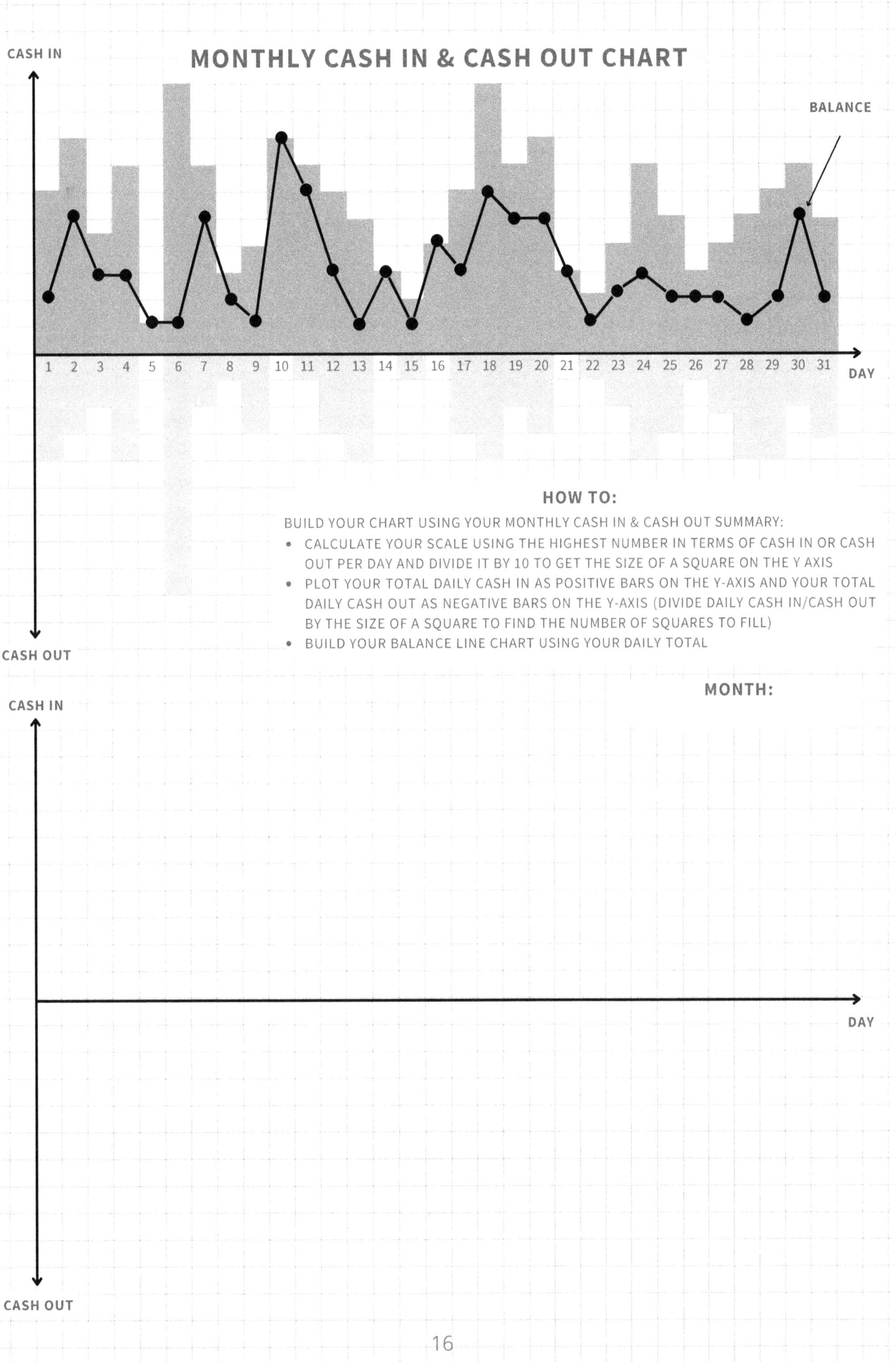
MONTHLY CASH IN & CASH OUT CHART
CASH IN
BALANCE
1 2 3 4 5 6 7 8 9 10 11 12 13 14 15 16 17 18 19 20 21 22 23 24 25 26 27 28 29 30 31
DAY
CASH OUT
HOW TO:
BUILD YOUR CHART USING YOUR MONTHLY CASH IN & CASH OUT SUMMARY:
• CALCULATE YOUR SCALE USING THE HIGHEST NUMBER IN TERMS OF CASH IN OR CASH OUT PER DAY AND DIVIDE IT BY 10 TO GET THE SIZE OF A SQUARE ON THE Y AXIS
• PLOT YOUR TOTAL DAILY CASH IN AS POSITIVE BARS ON THE Y-AXIS AND YOUR TOTAL DAILY CASH OUT AS NEGATIVE BARS ON THE Y-AXIS (DIVIDE DAILY CASH IN/CASH OUT BY THE SIZE OF A SQUARE TO FIND THE NUMBER OF SQUARES TO FILL)
• BUILD YOUR BALANCE LINE CHART USING YOUR DAILY TOTAL
MONTH:
CASH IN
DAY
CASH OUT

MONTHLY CASH IN & CASH OUT SUMMARY

MONTH : ....

DATE	DAY	CASH IN	CASH OUT	BALANCE	NOTES
1					
2					
3					
4					
5					
6					
7					
8					
9					
10					
11					
12					
13					
14					
15					
16					
17					
18					
19					
20					
21					
22					
23					
24					
25					
26					
27					
28					
29					
30					
31					
TOTAL					

MONTHLY CASH IN & CASH OUT CHART

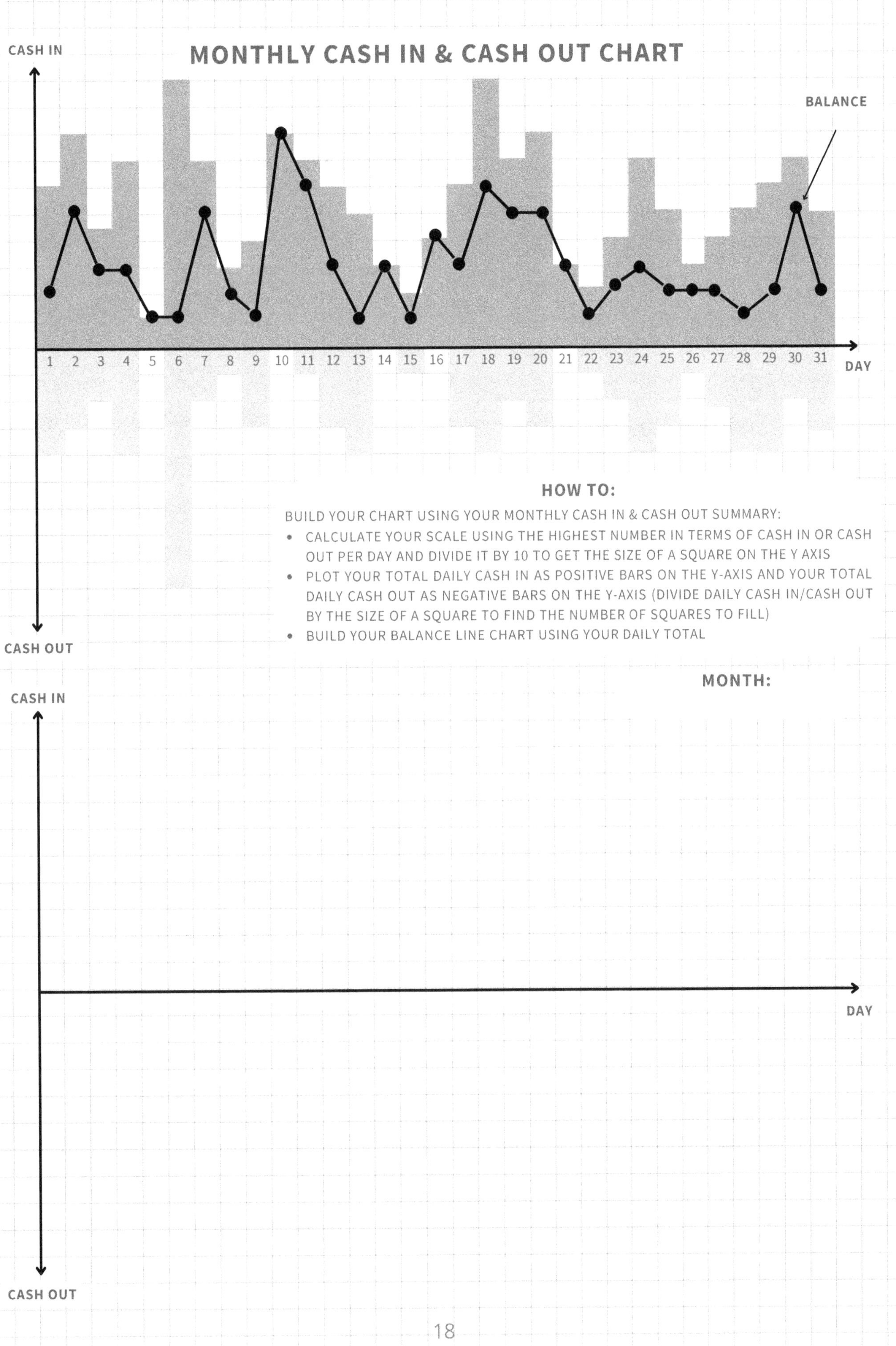

HOW TO:

BUILD YOUR CHART USING YOUR MONTHLY CASH IN & CASH OUT SUMMARY:

- CALCULATE YOUR SCALE USING THE HIGHEST NUMBER IN TERMS OF CASH IN OR CASH OUT PER DAY AND DIVIDE IT BY 10 TO GET THE SIZE OF A SQUARE ON THE Y AXIS
- PLOT YOUR TOTAL DAILY CASH IN AS POSITIVE BARS ON THE Y-AXIS AND YOUR TOTAL DAILY CASH OUT AS NEGATIVE BARS ON THE Y-AXIS (DIVIDE DAILY CASH IN/CASH OUT BY THE SIZE OF A SQUARE TO FIND THE NUMBER OF SQUARES TO FILL)
- BUILD YOUR BALANCE LINE CHART USING YOUR DAILY TOTAL

MONTH:

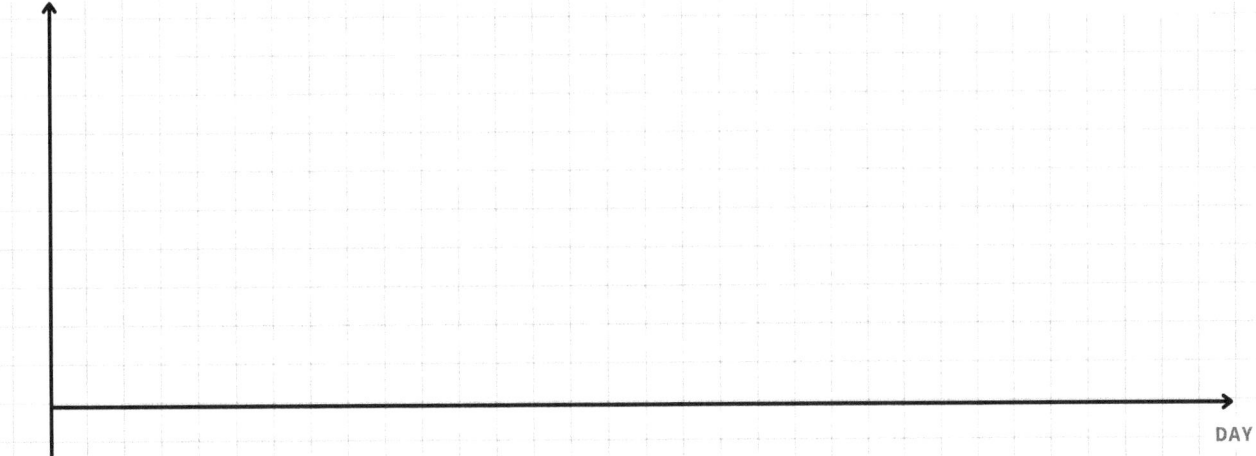

MONTHLY CASH IN & CASH OUT SUMMARY

MONTH : ....

DATE	DAY	CASH IN	CASH OUT	BALANCE	NOTES
1					
2					
3					
4					
5					
6					
7					
8					
9					
10					
11					
12					
13					
14					
15					
16					
17					
18					
19					
20					
21					
22					
23					
24					
25					
26					
27					
28					
29					
30					
31					
TOTAL					

MONTHLY CASH IN & CASH OUT CHART

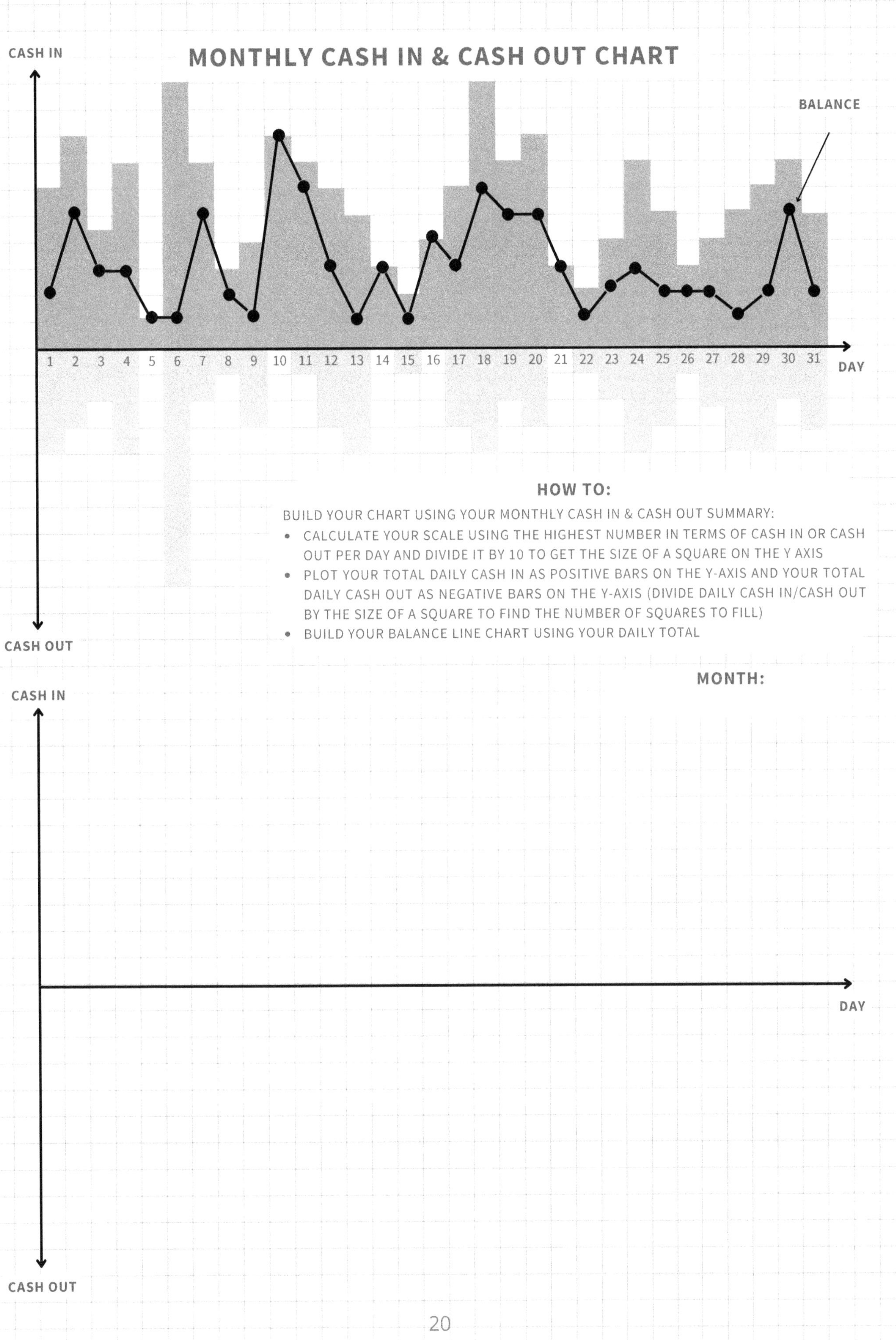

HOW TO:

BUILD YOUR CHART USING YOUR MONTHLY CASH IN & CASH OUT SUMMARY:

- CALCULATE YOUR SCALE USING THE HIGHEST NUMBER IN TERMS OF CASH IN OR CASH OUT PER DAY AND DIVIDE IT BY 10 TO GET THE SIZE OF A SQUARE ON THE Y AXIS
- PLOT YOUR TOTAL DAILY CASH IN AS POSITIVE BARS ON THE Y-AXIS AND YOUR TOTAL DAILY CASH OUT AS NEGATIVE BARS ON THE Y-AXIS (DIVIDE DAILY CASH IN/CASH OUT BY THE SIZE OF A SQUARE TO FIND THE NUMBER OF SQUARES TO FILL)
- BUILD YOUR BALANCE LINE CHART USING YOUR DAILY TOTAL

MONTHLY CASH IN & CASH OUT SUMMARY

MONTH : ....

DATE	DAY	CASH IN	CASH OUT	BALANCE	NOTES
1					
2					
3					
4					
5					
6					
7					
8					
9					
10					
11					
12					
13					
14					
15					
16					
17					
18					
19					
20					
21					
22					
23					
24					
25					
26					
27					
28					
29					
30					
31					
TOTAL					

MONTHLY CASH IN & CASH OUT CHART

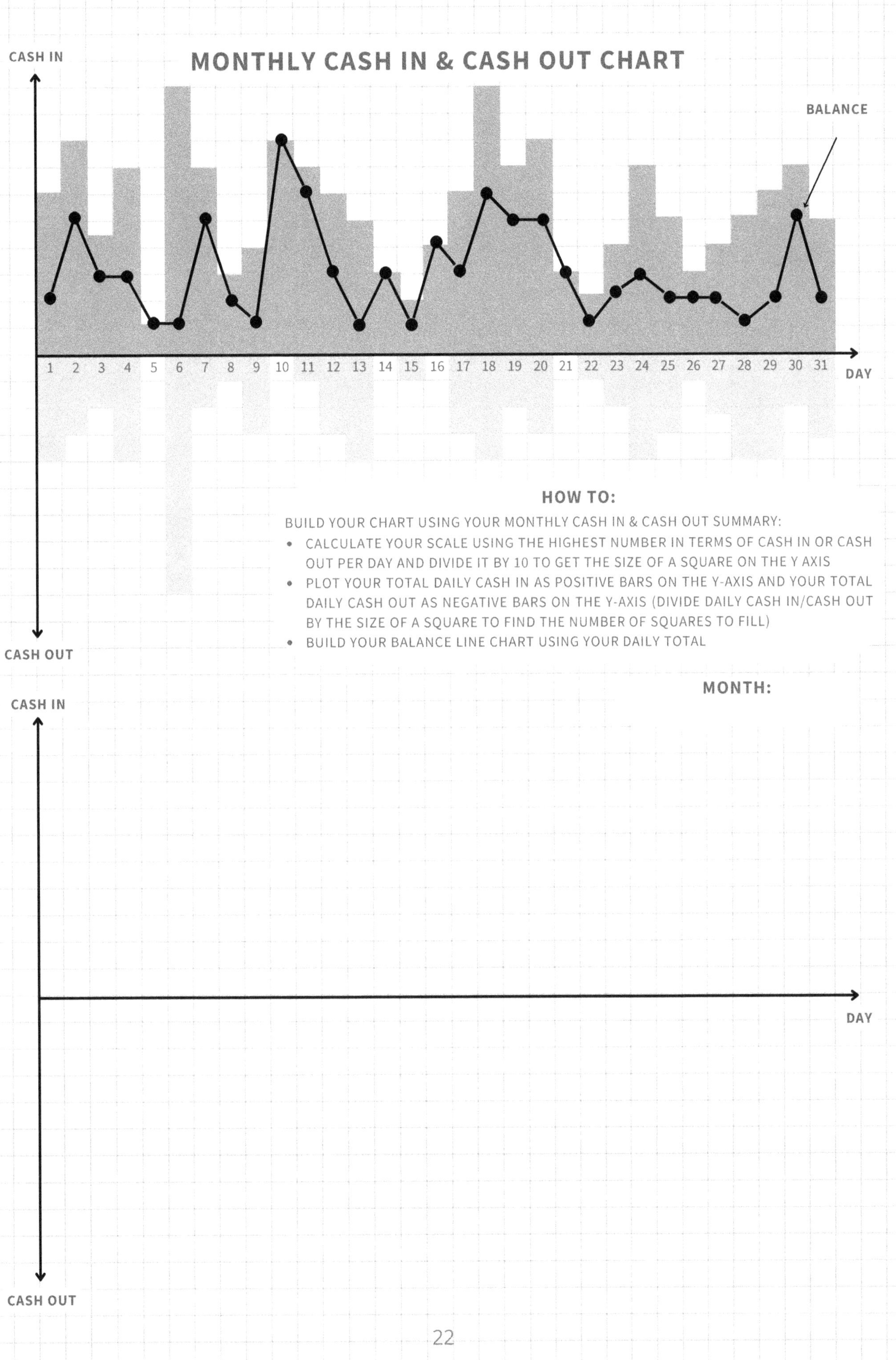

HOW TO:

BUILD YOUR CHART USING YOUR MONTHLY CASH IN & CASH OUT SUMMARY:

- CALCULATE YOUR SCALE USING THE HIGHEST NUMBER IN TERMS OF CASH IN OR CASH OUT PER DAY AND DIVIDE IT BY 10 TO GET THE SIZE OF A SQUARE ON THE Y AXIS
- PLOT YOUR TOTAL DAILY CASH IN AS POSITIVE BARS ON THE Y-AXIS AND YOUR TOTAL DAILY CASH OUT AS NEGATIVE BARS ON THE Y-AXIS (DIVIDE DAILY CASH IN/CASH OUT BY THE SIZE OF A SQUARE TO FIND THE NUMBER OF SQUARES TO FILL)
- BUILD YOUR BALANCE LINE CHART USING YOUR DAILY TOTAL

MONTH:

MONTHLY CASH IN & CASH OUT SUMMARY

MONTH : ....

DATE	DAY	CASH IN	CASH OUT	BALANCE	NOTES
1					
2					
3					
4					
5					
6					
7					
8					
9					
10					
11					
12					
13					
14					
15					
16					
17					
18					
19					
20					
21					
22					
23					
24					
25					
26					
27					
28					
29					
30					
31					
TOTAL					

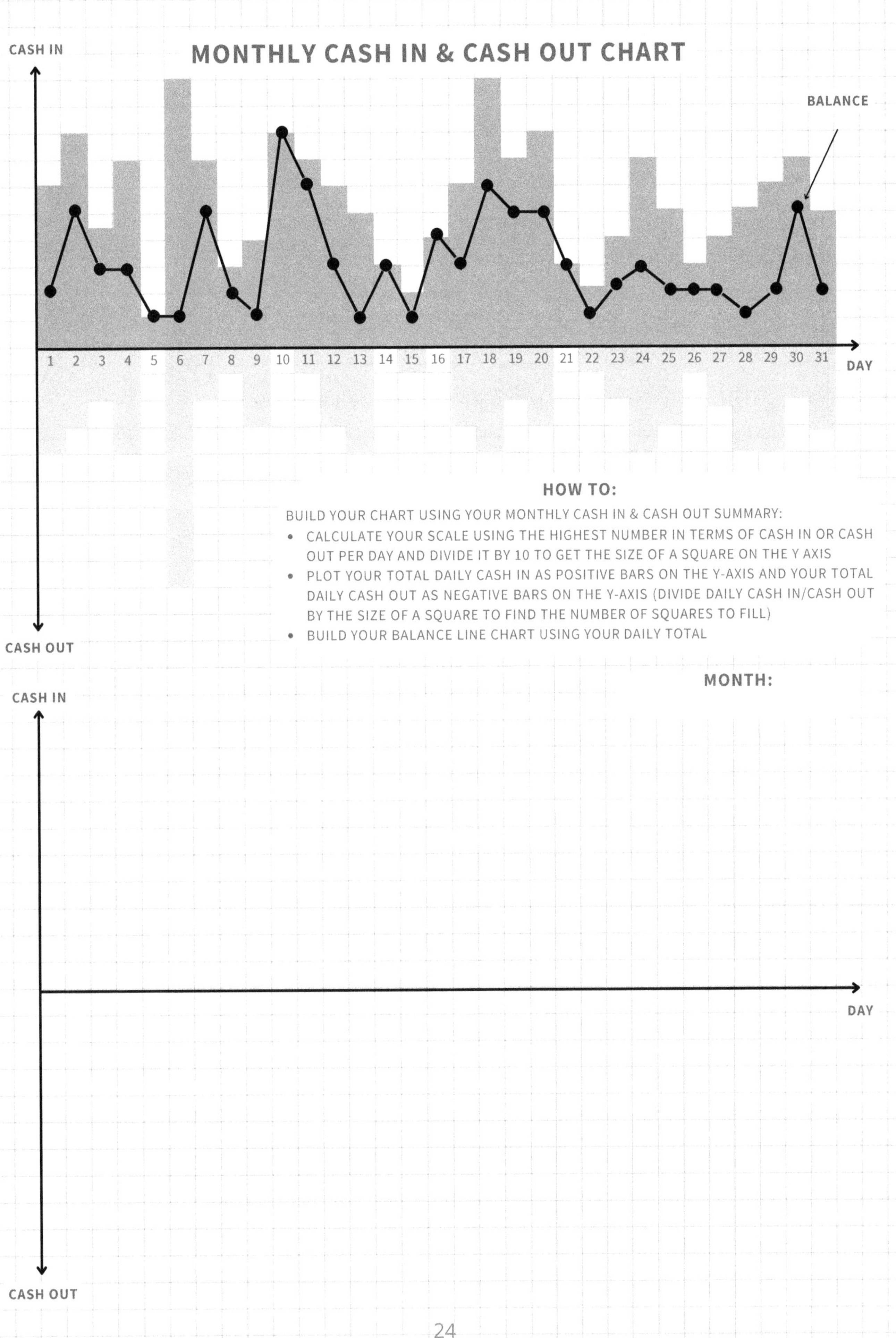

HOW TO:

BUILD YOUR CHART USING YOUR MONTHLY CASH IN & CASH OUT SUMMARY:

- CALCULATE YOUR SCALE USING THE HIGHEST NUMBER IN TERMS OF CASH IN OR CASH OUT PER DAY AND DIVIDE IT BY 10 TO GET THE SIZE OF A SQUARE ON THE Y AXIS
- PLOT YOUR TOTAL DAILY CASH IN AS POSITIVE BARS ON THE Y-AXIS AND YOUR TOTAL DAILY CASH OUT AS NEGATIVE BARS ON THE Y-AXIS (DIVIDE DAILY CASH IN/CASH OUT BY THE SIZE OF A SQUARE TO FIND THE NUMBER OF SQUARES TO FILL)
- BUILD YOUR BALANCE LINE CHART USING YOUR DAILY TOTAL

MONTH:

MONTHLY CASH IN & CASH OUT SUMMARY

MONTH : ....

DATE	DAY	CASH IN	CASH OUT	BALANCE	NOTES
1					
2					
3					
4					
5					
6					
7					
8					
9					
10					
11					
12					
13					
14					
15					
16					
17					
18					
19					
20					
21					
22					
23					
24					
25					
26					
27					
28					
29					
30					
31					
TOTAL					

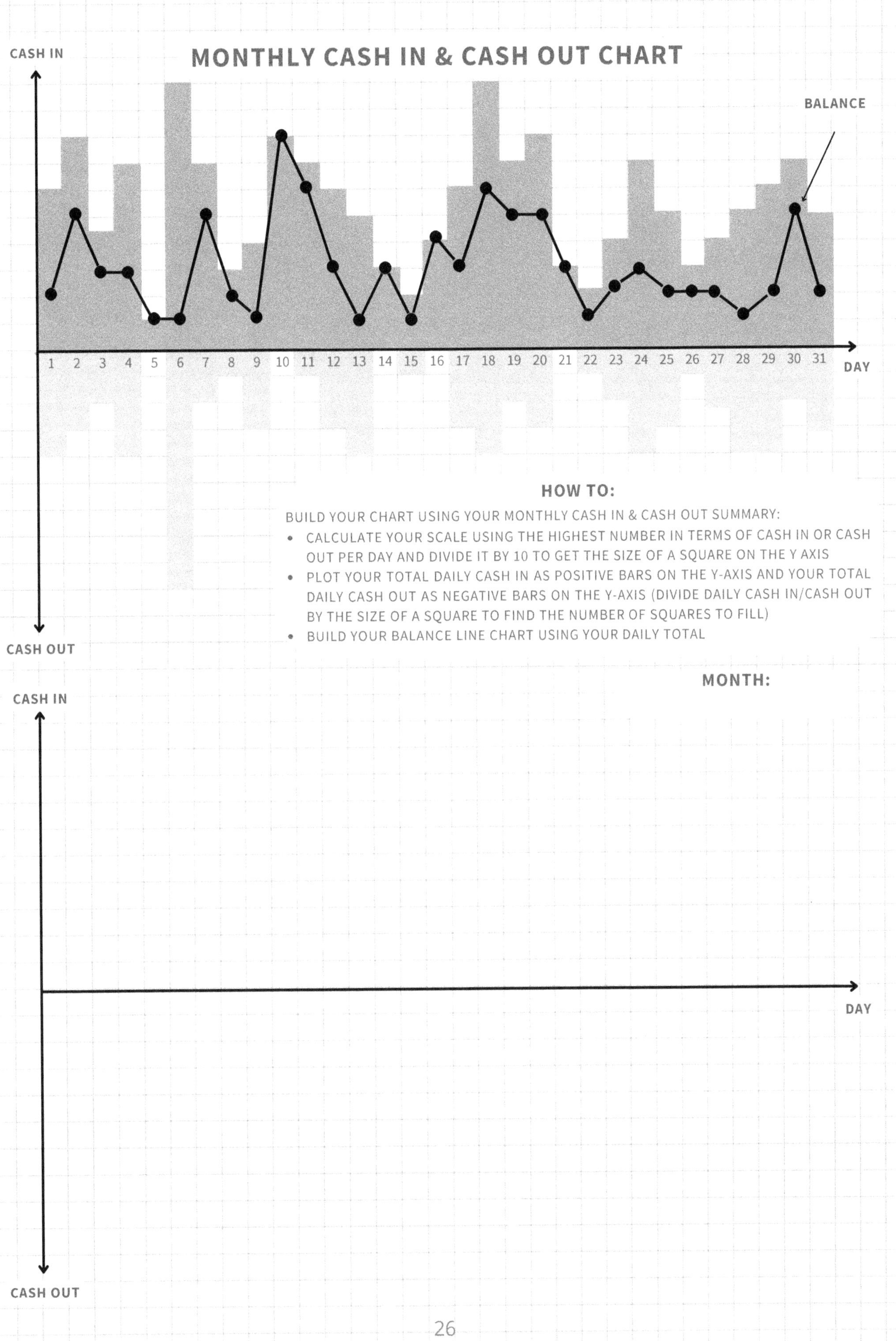

HOW TO:

BUILD YOUR CHART USING YOUR MONTHLY CASH IN & CASH OUT SUMMARY:

- CALCULATE YOUR SCALE USING THE HIGHEST NUMBER IN TERMS OF CASH IN OR CASH OUT PER DAY AND DIVIDE IT BY 10 TO GET THE SIZE OF A SQUARE ON THE Y AXIS
- PLOT YOUR TOTAL DAILY CASH IN AS POSITIVE BARS ON THE Y-AXIS AND YOUR TOTAL DAILY CASH OUT AS NEGATIVE BARS ON THE Y-AXIS (DIVIDE DAILY CASH IN/CASH OUT BY THE SIZE OF A SQUARE TO FIND THE NUMBER OF SQUARES TO FILL)
- BUILD YOUR BALANCE LINE CHART USING YOUR DAILY TOTAL

MONTH:

DAILY CASH IN & CASH OUT

DATE FROM: .... **TO:** .... **PREV.BALANCE:** ....

DATE	DESCRIPTION	CASH IN	CASH OUT	BALANCE
TOTAL				

DATE: .... **SIGNED:**

DAILY CASH IN & CASH OUT

DATE FROM: ____________ TO: ____________ PREV.BALANCE: ____________

DATE	DESCRIPTION	CASH IN	CASH OUT	BALANCE
TOTAL				

DATE: ____________ SIGNED:

DAILY CASH IN & CASH OUT

DATE FROM: ______________ **TO:** ______________ **PREV.BALANCE:** ______________

DATE	DESCRIPTION	CASH IN	CASH OUT	BALANCE
TOTAL				

DATE: ______________ **SIGNED:**

DAILY CASH IN & CASH OUT

DATE FROM: ______________ TO: ______________ PREV.BALANCE: ______________

DATE	DESCRIPTION	CASH IN	CASH OUT	BALANCE
TOTAL				

DATE: ______________ SIGNED:

DAILY CASH IN & CASH OUT

DATE FROM: ____________ TO: ____________ PREV.BALANCE: ____________

DATE	DESCRIPTION	CASH IN	CASH OUT	BALANCE
TOTAL				

DATE: ____________ SIGNED:

DAILY CASH IN & CASH OUT

DATE FROM: ______________ TO: ______________ PREV.BALANCE: ______________

DATE	DESCRIPTION	CASH IN	CASH OUT	BALANCE
TOTAL				

DATE: ______________ SIGNED:

DAILY CASH IN & CASH OUT

DATE FROM: ____________ TO: ____________ PREV.BALANCE: ____________

DATE	DESCRIPTION	CASH IN	CASH OUT	BALANCE
TOTAL				

DATE: ____________ SIGNED:

DAILY CASH IN & CASH OUT

DATE FROM: ____________ TO: ____________ PREV.BALANCE: ____________

DATE	DESCRIPTION	CASH IN	CASH OUT	BALANCE
TOTAL				

DATE: ____________ SIGNED:

DAILY CASH IN & CASH OUT

DATE FROM: ________________ TO: ________________ PREV.BALANCE: ________________

DATE	DESCRIPTION	CASH IN	CASH OUT	BALANCE
TOTAL				

DATE: ________________ SIGNED:

DAILY CASH IN & CASH OUT

DATE FROM: ______________ **TO:** ______________ **PREV.BALANCE:** ______________

DATE	DESCRIPTION	CASH IN	CASH OUT	BALANCE
TOTAL				

DATE: ______________ **SIGNED:**

DAILY CASH IN & CASH OUT

DATE FROM: ______________ TO: ______________ PREV.BALANCE: ______________

DATE	DESCRIPTION	CASH IN	CASH OUT	BALANCE
TOTAL				

DATE: ______________ SIGNED:

DAILY CASH IN & CASH OUT

DATE FROM: ______________ TO: ______________ PREV.BALANCE: ______________

DATE	DESCRIPTION	CASH IN	CASH OUT	BALANCE
TOTAL				

DATE: ______________ SIGNED:

DAILY CASH IN & CASH OUT

DATE FROM: .... TO: .... PREV.BALANCE: ....

DATE	DESCRIPTION	CASH IN	CASH OUT	BALANCE
TOTAL				

DATE: .... SIGNED:

DAILY CASH IN & CASH OUT

DATE FROM: ______________ TO: ______________ PREV.BALANCE: ______________

DATE	DESCRIPTION	CASH IN	CASH OUT	BALANCE
TOTAL				

DATE: ______________ SIGNED:

DAILY CASH IN & CASH OUT

DATE FROM: ______________ TO: ______________ PREV.BALANCE: ______________

DATE	DESCRIPTION	CASH IN	CASH OUT	BALANCE
TOTAL				

DATE: ______________ SIGNED:

DAILY CASH IN & CASH OUT

DATE FROM: ______________ **TO:** ______________ **PREV.BALANCE:** ______________

DATE	DESCRIPTION	CASH IN	CASH OUT	BALANCE
TOTAL				

DATE: ______________ **SIGNED:**

DAILY CASH IN & CASH OUT

DATE FROM: ____________ **TO:** ____________ **PREV.BALANCE:** ____________

DATE	DESCRIPTION	CASH IN	CASH OUT	BALANCE
TOTAL				

DATE: ____________ **SIGNED:**

DAILY CASH IN & CASH OUT

DATE FROM: ______________ TO: ______________ PREV.BALANCE: ______________

DATE	DESCRIPTION	CASH IN	CASH OUT	BALANCE
TOTAL				

DATE: ______________ SIGNED:

DAILY CASH IN & CASH OUT

DATE FROM: ______________ **TO:** ______________ **PREV.BALANCE:** ______________

DATE	DESCRIPTION	CASH IN	CASH OUT	BALANCE
TOTAL				

DATE: ______________ **SIGNED:**

DAILY CASH IN & CASH OUT

DATE FROM: ______________ TO: ______________ PREV.BALANCE: ______________

DATE	DESCRIPTION	CASH IN	CASH OUT	BALANCE
TOTAL				

DATE: ______________ SIGNED:

DAILY CASH IN & CASH OUT

DATE FROM: ____________ TO: ____________ PREV.BALANCE: ____________

DATE	DESCRIPTION	CASH IN	CASH OUT	BALANCE
TOTAL				

DATE: ____________ SIGNED:

DAILY CASH IN & CASH OUT

DATE FROM: ______________ TO: ______________ PREV.BALANCE: ______________

DATE	DESCRIPTION	CASH IN	CASH OUT	BALANCE
TOTAL				

DATE: ______________ SIGNED:

DAILY CASH IN & CASH OUT

DATE FROM: ______________ TO: ______________ PREV.BALANCE: ______________

DATE	DESCRIPTION	CASH IN	CASH OUT	BALANCE
TOTAL				

DATE: ______________ SIGNED:

DAILY CASH IN & CASH OUT

DATE FROM: ______________ TO: ______________ PREV.BALANCE: ______________

DATE	DESCRIPTION	CASH IN	CASH OUT	BALANCE
TOTAL				

DATE: ______________ SIGNED:

DAILY CASH IN & CASH OUT

DATE FROM: ____________	TO: ____________	PREV.BALANCE: ____________

DATE	DESCRIPTION	CASH IN	CASH OUT	BALANCE
TOTAL				

DATE: ____________ SIGNED:

DAILY CASH IN & CASH OUT

DATE FROM: ______________ TO: ______________ PREV.BALANCE: ______________

DATE	DESCRIPTION	CASH IN	CASH OUT	BALANCE
TOTAL				

DATE: ______________ SIGNED:

DAILY CASH IN & CASH OUT

DATE FROM: ____________ TO: ____________ PREV.BALANCE: ____________

DATE	DESCRIPTION	CASH IN	CASH OUT	BALANCE
TOTAL				

DATE: ____________ SIGNED:

DAILY CASH IN & CASH OUT

DATE FROM: ______________ TO: ______________ PREV.BALANCE: ______________

DATE	DESCRIPTION	CASH IN	CASH OUT	BALANCE
TOTAL				

DATE: ______________ SIGNED:

DAILY CASH IN & CASH OUT

DATE FROM: .... TO: .... PREV.BALANCE: ....

DATE	DESCRIPTION	CASH IN	CASH OUT	BALANCE
TOTAL				

DATE: .... SIGNED:

DAILY CASH IN & CASH OUT

DATE FROM: .... TO: .... PREV.BALANCE: ....

DATE	DESCRIPTION	CASH IN	CASH OUT	BALANCE
TOTAL				

DATE: .... SIGNED:

DAILY CASH IN & CASH OUT

DATE FROM: ____________ TO: ____________ PREV.BALANCE: ____________

DATE	DESCRIPTION	CASH IN	CASH OUT	BALANCE
TOTAL				

DATE: ____________ SIGNED:

DAILY CASH IN & CASH OUT

DATE FROM: ______________ TO: ______________ PREV.BALANCE: ______________

DATE	DESCRIPTION	CASH IN	CASH OUT	BALANCE
TOTAL				

DATE: ______________ SIGNED:

DAILY CASH IN & CASH OUT

DATE FROM: ____________ **TO:** ____________ **PREV.BALANCE:** ____________

DATE	DESCRIPTION	CASH IN	CASH OUT	BALANCE
TOTAL				

DATE: ____________ **SIGNED:**

DAILY CASH IN & CASH OUT

DATE FROM: ____________ TO: ____________ PREV.BALANCE: ____________

DATE	DESCRIPTION	CASH IN	CASH OUT	BALANCE
TOTAL				

DATE: ____________ SIGNED:

DAILY CASH IN & CASH OUT

DATE FROM: ____________ TO: ____________ PREV.BALANCE: ____________

DATE	DESCRIPTION	CASH IN	CASH OUT	BALANCE
TOTAL				

DATE: ____________ SIGNED:

DAILY CASH IN & CASH OUT

DATE FROM: ______________ TO: ______________ PREV.BALANCE: ______________

DATE	DESCRIPTION	CASH IN	CASH OUT	BALANCE
TOTAL				

DATE: ______________ SIGNED:

DAILY CASH IN & CASH OUT

DATE FROM: .... TO: .... PREV.BALANCE: ....

DATE	DESCRIPTION	CASH IN	CASH OUT	BALANCE
TOTAL				

DATE: .... SIGNED:

DAILY CASH IN & CASH OUT

DATE FROM: ______________ TO: ______________ PREV.BALANCE: ______________

DATE	DESCRIPTION	CASH IN	CASH OUT	BALANCE
TOTAL				

DATE: ______________ SIGNED:

DAILY CASH IN & CASH OUT

DATE FROM: ____________ TO: ____________ PREV.BALANCE: ____________

DATE	DESCRIPTION	CASH IN	CASH OUT	BALANCE
TOTAL				

DATE: ____________ SIGNED:

DAILY CASH IN & CASH OUT

DATE FROM: ______________ TO: ______________ PREV.BALANCE: ______________

DATE	DESCRIPTION	CASH IN	CASH OUT	BALANCE
TOTAL				

DATE: ______________ SIGNED:

DAILY CASH IN & CASH OUT

DATE FROM: ______________ **TO:** ______________ **PREV.BALANCE:** ______________

DATE	DESCRIPTION	CASH IN	CASH OUT	BALANCE
TOTAL				

DATE: ______________ **SIGNED:**

DAILY CASH IN & CASH OUT

DATE FROM: .... TO: .... PREV.BALANCE: ....

DATE	DESCRIPTION	CASH IN	CASH OUT	BALANCE
TOTAL				

DATE: .... SIGNED:

DAILY CASH IN & CASH OUT

DATE FROM: .... TO: .... PREV.BALANCE: ....

DATE	DESCRIPTION	CASH IN	CASH OUT	BALANCE
TOTAL				

DATE: ....

SIGNED:

DAILY CASH IN & CASH OUT

DATE FROM: .... TO: .... PREV.BALANCE: ....

DATE	DESCRIPTION	CASH IN	CASH OUT	BALANCE
TOTAL				

DATE: .... SIGNED:

DAILY CASH IN & CASH OUT

DATE FROM: ______________ TO: ______________ PREV.BALANCE: ______________

DATE	DESCRIPTION	CASH IN	CASH OUT	BALANCE
TOTAL				

DATE: ______________ SIGNED:

DAILY CASH IN & CASH OUT

DATE FROM: ____________ **TO:** ____________ **PREV.BALANCE:** ____________

DATE	DESCRIPTION	CASH IN	CASH OUT	BALANCE
TOTAL				

DATE: ____________ **SIGNED:**

DAILY CASH IN & CASH OUT

DATE FROM: ______________ TO: ______________ PREV.BALANCE: ______________

DATE	DESCRIPTION	CASH IN	CASH OUT	BALANCE
TOTAL				

DATE: ______________ SIGNED:

DAILY CASH IN & CASH OUT

DATE FROM: ______________ TO: ______________ PREV.BALANCE: ______________

DATE	DESCRIPTION	CASH IN	CASH OUT	BALANCE
TOTAL				

DATE: ______________ SIGNED:

DAILY CASH IN & CASH OUT

DATE FROM: ____________ TO: ____________ PREV.BALANCE: ____________

DATE	DESCRIPTION	CASH IN	CASH OUT	BALANCE
TOTAL				

DATE: ____________ SIGNED:

DAILY CASH IN & CASH OUT

DATE FROM: ______________ TO: ______________ PREV.BALANCE: ______________

DATE	DESCRIPTION	CASH IN	CASH OUT	BALANCE
TOTAL				

DATE: ______________ SIGNED:

DAILY CASH IN & CASH OUT

DATE FROM: .... TO: .... PREV.BALANCE: ....

DATE	DESCRIPTION	CASH IN	CASH OUT	BALANCE
TOTAL				

DATE: .... SIGNED:

DAILY CASH IN & CASH OUT

DATE FROM: ______________ TO: ______________ PREV.BALANCE: ______________

DATE	DESCRIPTION	CASH IN	CASH OUT	BALANCE
TOTAL				

DATE: ______________ SIGNED:

DAILY CASH IN & CASH OUT

DATE FROM: ____________ **TO:** ____________ **PREV.BALANCE:** ____________

DATE	DESCRIPTION	CASH IN	CASH OUT	BALANCE
TOTAL				

DATE: ____________ **SIGNED:**

DAILY CASH IN & CASH OUT

DATE FROM: ______________ TO: ______________ PREV.BALANCE: ______________

DATE	DESCRIPTION	CASH IN	CASH OUT	BALANCE
TOTAL				

DATE: ______________ SIGNED:

DAILY CASH IN & CASH OUT

DATE FROM: ____________ TO: ____________ PREV.BALANCE: ____________

DATE	DESCRIPTION	CASH IN	CASH OUT	BALANCE
TOTAL				
DATE: ____________		SIGNED:		

DAILY CASH IN & CASH OUT

DATE FROM: ____________ TO: ____________ PREV.BALANCE: ____________

DATE	DESCRIPTION	CASH IN	CASH OUT	BALANCE
TOTAL				

DATE: ____________ SIGNED:

DAILY CASH IN & CASH OUT

DATE FROM: .... TO: .... PREV.BALANCE: ....

DATE	DESCRIPTION	CASH IN	CASH OUT	BALANCE
TOTAL				

DATE: .... SIGNED:

DAILY CASH IN & CASH OUT

DATE FROM: .... TO: .... PREV.BALANCE: ....

DATE	DESCRIPTION	CASH IN	CASH OUT	BALANCE
TOTAL				

DATE: .... SIGNED:

DAILY CASH IN & CASH OUT

DATE FROM: ______________ TO: ______________ PREV.BALANCE: ______________

DATE	DESCRIPTION	CASH IN	CASH OUT	BALANCE
TOTAL				

DATE: ______________ SIGNED:

DAILY CASH IN & CASH OUT

DATE FROM: .... TO: .... PREV.BALANCE: ....

DATE	DESCRIPTION	CASH IN	CASH OUT	BALANCE
TOTAL				

DATE: .... SIGNED:

DAILY CASH IN & CASH OUT

DATE FROM: ______________ TO: ______________ PREV.BALANCE: ______________

DATE	DESCRIPTION	CASH IN	CASH OUT	BALANCE
TOTAL				

DATE: ______________ SIGNED:

DAILY CASH IN & CASH OUT

DATE FROM: ______________ TO: ______________ PREV.BALANCE: ______________

DATE	DESCRIPTION	CASH IN	CASH OUT	BALANCE
TOTAL				

DATE: ______________ SIGNED:

DAILY CASH IN & CASH OUT

DATE FROM: .... TO: .... PREV.BALANCE: ....

DATE	DESCRIPTION	CASH IN	CASH OUT	BALANCE
TOTAL				

DATE: .... SIGNED:

DAILY CASH IN & CASH OUT

DATE FROM: .... TO: .... PREV.BALANCE: ....

DATE	DESCRIPTION	CASH IN	CASH OUT	BALANCE
TOTAL				

DATE: .... SIGNED:

DAILY CASH IN & CASH OUT

DATE FROM: ____________ TO: ____________ PREV.BALANCE: ____________

DATE	DESCRIPTION	CASH IN	CASH OUT	BALANCE
TOTAL				

DATE: ____________ SIGNED:

DAILY CASH IN & CASH OUT

DATE FROM: ____________ TO: ____________ PREV.BALANCE: ____________

DATE	DESCRIPTION	CASH IN	CASH OUT	BALANCE
TOTAL				

DATE: ____________ SIGNED:

DAILY CASH IN & CASH OUT

DATE FROM: ____________ TO: ____________ PREV.BALANCE: ____________

DATE	DESCRIPTION	CASH IN	CASH OUT	BALANCE
TOTAL				

DATE: ____________ SIGNED:

DAILY CASH IN & CASH OUT

DATE FROM: ____________ TO: ____________ PREV.BALANCE: ____________

DATE	DESCRIPTION	CASH IN	CASH OUT	BALANCE
TOTAL				

DATE: ____________ SIGNED:

DAILY CASH IN & CASH OUT

DATE FROM: ______________ TO: ______________ PREV.BALANCE: ______________

DATE	DESCRIPTION	CASH IN	CASH OUT	BALANCE
TOTAL				

DATE: ______________ SIGNED:

DAILY CASH IN & CASH OUT

DATE FROM: .... TO: .... PREV.BALANCE: ....

DATE	DESCRIPTION	CASH IN	CASH OUT	BALANCE
TOTAL				

DATE: .... SIGNED:

DAILY CASH IN & CASH OUT

DATE FROM: .... TO: .... PREV.BALANCE: ....

DATE	DESCRIPTION	CASH IN	CASH OUT	BALANCE
TOTAL				

DATE: .... SIGNED:

DAILY CASH IN & CASH OUT

DATE FROM: .... TO: .... PREV.BALANCE: ....

DATE	DESCRIPTION	CASH IN	CASH OUT	BALANCE
TOTAL				

DATE: .... SIGNED:

DAILY CASH IN & CASH OUT

DATE FROM: ____________ **TO:** ____________ **PREV.BALANCE:** ____________

DATE	DESCRIPTION	CASH IN	CASH OUT	BALANCE
TOTAL				

DATE: ____________ **SIGNED:**

DAILY CASH IN & CASH OUT

DATE FROM: ______________ TO: ______________ PREV.BALANCE: ______________

DATE	DESCRIPTION	CASH IN	CASH OUT	BALANCE
TOTAL				

DATE: ______________ SIGNED:

DAILY CASH IN & CASH OUT

DATE FROM: ____________ **TO:** ____________ **PREV.BALANCE:** ____________

DATE	DESCRIPTION	CASH IN	CASH OUT	BALANCE
TOTAL				

DATE: ____________ **SIGNED:**

DAILY CASH IN & CASH OUT

DATE FROM: ____________ TO: ____________ PREV.BALANCE: ____________

DATE	DESCRIPTION	CASH IN	CASH OUT	BALANCE
TOTAL				

DATE: ____________ SIGNED:

DAILY CASH IN & CASH OUT

DATE FROM: .... **TO:** .... **PREV.BALANCE:** ....

DATE	DESCRIPTION	CASH IN	CASH OUT	BALANCE
TOTAL				

DATE: .... **SIGNED:**

DAILY CASH IN & CASH OUT

DATE FROM: ______________ TO: ______________ PREV.BALANCE: ______________

DATE	DESCRIPTION	CASH IN	CASH OUT	BALANCE
TOTAL				

DATE: ______________ SIGNED:

DAILY CASH IN & CASH OUT

DATE FROM: ____________ TO: ____________ PREV.BALANCE: ____________

DATE	DESCRIPTION	CASH IN	CASH OUT	BALANCE
TOTAL				

DATE: ____________ SIGNED:

DAILY CASH IN & CASH OUT

DATE FROM: ______________ TO: ______________ PREV.BALANCE: ______________

DATE	DESCRIPTION	CASH IN	CASH OUT	BALANCE
TOTAL				

DATE: ______________ SIGNED:

DAILY CASH IN & CASH OUT

DATE FROM: ____________ TO: ____________ PREV.BALANCE: ____________

DATE	DESCRIPTION	CASH IN	CASH OUT	BALANCE
TOTAL				

DATE: ____________ SIGNED:

DAILY CASH IN & CASH OUT

DATE FROM: .... TO: .... PREV.BALANCE: ....

DATE	DESCRIPTION	CASH IN	CASH OUT	BALANCE
TOTAL				

DATE: .... SIGNED:

DAILY CASH IN & CASH OUT

DATE FROM: ____________ TO: ____________ PREV.BALANCE: ____________

DATE	DESCRIPTION	CASH IN	CASH OUT	BALANCE
TOTAL				

DATE: ____________ SIGNED:

DAILY CASH IN & CASH OUT

DATE FROM: ______________ TO: ______________ PREV.BALANCE: ______________

DATE	DESCRIPTION	CASH IN	CASH OUT	BALANCE
TOTAL				

DATE: ______________ SIGNED:

DAILY CASH IN & CASH OUT

DATE FROM: ______________ TO: ______________ PREV.BALANCE: ______________

DATE	DESCRIPTION	CASH IN	CASH OUT	BALANCE
TOTAL				

DATE: ______________ SIGNED:

DAILY CASH IN & CASH OUT

DATE FROM: ____________ TO: ____________ PREV.BALANCE: ____________

DATE	DESCRIPTION	CASH IN	CASH OUT	BALANCE
TOTAL				

DATE: ____________ SIGNED:

DAILY CASH IN & CASH OUT

DATE FROM: ____________ TO: ____________ PREV.BALANCE: ____________

DATE	DESCRIPTION	CASH IN	CASH OUT	BALANCE
TOTAL				

DATE: ____________ SIGNED:

DAILY CASH IN & CASH OUT

DATE FROM: ______________ TO: ______________ PREV.BALANCE: ______________

DATE	DESCRIPTION	CASH IN	CASH OUT	BALANCE
TOTAL				

DATE: ______________ SIGNED:

DAILY CASH IN & CASH OUT

DATE FROM: ____________ **TO:** ____________ **PREV.BALANCE:** ____________

DATE	DESCRIPTION	CASH IN	CASH OUT	BALANCE
TOTAL				

DATE: ____________ **SIGNED:**

DAILY CASH IN & CASH OUT

DATE FROM: .... TO: .... PREV.BALANCE: ....

DATE	DESCRIPTION	CASH IN	CASH OUT	BALANCE
TOTAL				

DATE: .... SIGNED:

www.ingramcontent.com/pod-product-compliance
Lightning Source LLC
Chambersburg PA
CBHW051758200326
41597CB00025B/4597
* 9 7 8 1 8 0 3 9 3 2 1 4 9 *